FLINT WATER CRISIS

UNNATURAL DISASTERS

FLINT WATER PLANT

JULIE KNUTSON

Published in the United States of America by Cherry Lake Publishing Group
Ann Arbor, Michigan
www.cherrylakepublishing.com

Reading Adviser: Marla Conn, MS, Ed., Literacy specialist, Read-Ability, Inc.
Photo Credits: © Linda Parton/Shutterstock.com, front cover, 1, 14; © AYDO8/Shutterstock.com, 5;
    © Pacific Press Media Production Corp./Alamy Stock Photo, 6; © ZUMA Press Inc/Alamy Stock Photo, 8;
    © History and Art Collection/Alamy Stock Photo, 11; © Courtesy Library of Congress, LC-USF34-040027-D, 12;
    © Brand Diverse Solutions Steven Barber/iStock.com, 17; © Jim West/Alamy Stock Photo, 18, 20, 22;
    © Jeff Kowalsky/AP/Shutterstock.com; © REUTERS/Alamy Stock Photo, 26

Cherry Lake Press is an imprint of Cherry Lake Publishing Group.

Library of Congress Cataloging-in-Publication Data
Names: Knutson, Julie, author.
Title: Flint water crisis / Julie Knutson.
Description: Ann Arbor, Michigan : Cherry Lake Publishing, 2021. | Series: Unnatural disasters : human
    error, design flaws, and bad decisions | Includes index. | Audience: Grades 4-6 | Summary: "Human
    modification of the environment always carries a risk of accident and folly. Explore the causes and
    consequences of the devastating water crisis in Flint, Michigan. Guided by compelling questions such
    as, "What led to this disaster?," "Who was impacted by it?," and "What changed in its aftermath?" the
    interdisciplinary content blends social studies and science. Ultimately, it pushes students to consider
    how humans can meet their need for resources in a safe, sustainable way. Books include table of
    contents, index, glossary, author biography, and timeline"–Provided by publisher.
Identifiers: LCCN 2020040001 (print) | LCCN 2020040002 (ebook) | ISBN 9781534180208 (hardcover) |
    ISBN 9781534181915 (paperback) | ISBN 9781534181212 (pdf) | ISBN 9781534181915 (ebook)
Subjects: LCSH: Drinking water—Contamination—Michigan—Flint—Juvenile literature. | Lead—
    Environmental aspects—Michigan—Flint—Juvenile literature. | Water quality management—Michigan—
    Flint—Juvenile literature.
Classification: LCC TD225.F57 K58 2021 (print) | LCC TD225.F57 (ebook) |
    DDC 363.6/10977437—dc23
LC record available at https://lccn.loc.gov/2020040001
LC ebook record available at https://lccn.loc.gov/2020040002

Cherry Lake Publishing Group would like to acknowledge the work of the Partnership for 21st Century
Learning, a Network of Battelle for Kids. Please visit http://www.battelleforkids.org/networks/p21
for more information.

Printed in the United States of America
Corporate Graphics

ABOUT THE AUTHOR

Julie Knutson is an Illinois-based author. In her spare moments, she enjoys investigating
new places and ideas alongside her husband, son, and border collie.

TABLE OF CONTENTS

INTRODUCTION

On April 13, 2014, the headline of an editorial in the *Flint Journal* made a bold proclamation: "Switch to Flint River Water Represents New Era in Flint." Residents in this Michigan city best known for making GMC trucks had no idea how true that statement would turn out to be. But it didn't end up being the "virtually unnoticeable" changeover promised in the editorial. It also wasn't the "good temporary solution" that the newspaper foresaw. Instead, the new water source brought about a major public health disaster. Its aftershocks are still felt today.

There are many factors that could cause tap water to change color.

The environmental justice movement began in the United States in the 1970s. It calls for an end to environmental racism, where communities of color are more impacted by environmental hazards.

For 18 long months, Flint's citizens battled to have local and state officials recognize what they knew each time they turned on their taps: something was wrong with their water. In color, the water could be mistaken for iced tea or even coffee. It had a strong smell and a chemical taste. On top of that, residents who bathed in it experienced odd problems. Rashes and hair loss were common. One woman's eyelashes fell out. Inside their bodies, too, many people felt different after the switch. Neighbors compared complaints of headaches, stomachaches, joint pain, and lack of energy.

Yes, something was definitely wrong with the water. But what exactly was it?

Access to clean water is a basic human right. In its Sustainable Development Goals, the United Nations (UN) calls "Clean Water and Sanitation" a global priority. Equal access to quality water is so important that the UN named the years 2018 to 2028 the Water Action Decade.

Flint community members organize together at local churches and other community areas.

It took months of community activists fighting for testing to identify the issue. Because the state government refused to see and hear their plight, organizers turned to environmental scientists and doctors for help. These citizen scientists teamed up with experts to reveal the truth. Toxic levels of **lead** and other metals, along with life-threatening bacteria had turned the water into poison. And it was caused by old, **leaching** pipes. Water—something that every person on earth needs to survive—couldn't be trusted as safe.

Who and what caused this unnatural disaster? How did it impact the people of Flint, and how did they fight to make themselves visible? What actions have been taken to fix the problem? And what does the future hold for Flint with its aging **infrastructure**, budget problems, and shrinking population?

Environmental justice is based on two core ideas. One is that community members should have a say in decisions that impact their health and well-being. The other is that no groups should be disproportionately harmed by pollution or waste. In the case of Flint, both of these core ideas were violated. The community wasn't involved in the decision-making process. And Flint's majority African American population and residents living in poorer neighborhoods were more affected by the crisis than middle- and upper-income White people.

CHAPTER 1

Before

Throughout the first part of the 20th century, Flint was known as a prosperous, growing city. A February 12, 1950, article in the *Detroit Free Press* marveled at the wealth and good fortune of the community. Titled "GM City Sets Pace for State: Hard-Working Flint Has Struck It Rich," the story noted high incomes and housing shortages. In the view of the reporter and many other observers, Flint was standing "on a new plateau of prosperity."

You wouldn't think fresh water would ever be an issue in Michigan. The Great Lakes surrounding the state contain one-fifth of the world's freshwater. Michigan's coastline stretches 3,200 miles (5,150 kilometers), more than any other state except Alaska.

This is Detroit + Saginaw Street. May the 1 1904
Good By
Linnie

The current "Vehicle City" arch is a replica of one that existed in Flint during the early 1900s.

Flint was settled by fur traders in the 19th century. Its location along the Flint River, its position between Detroit and Saginaw, and its abundant **natural resources** made it an ideal spot for a trading post. Soon, lumber milled from the surrounding forests became the town's main industry. Out of that grew a thriving carriage-making industry. This evolved into auto manufacturing in the early 20th century. Soon, Flint was proudly known by its nickname "Vehicle City."

The 1937 United Auto Workers sit-down strike at General Motors lasted 44 days.

General Motors, or GM, was the economic engine that drove the city. But in the second half of the century, the automotive company **downsized** its operations. Unemployed workers looked outside of Flint for work. Businesses were losing customers, and they too packed up and left town. Social conditions also changed. Many White residents left when laws changed the racial makeup of their neighborhoods. Flint's population dropped 18 percent between 2000 and 2010. That meant there were fewer people to pay into the larger pool for essential services like schools, waste collection,

Community Organizing across the Decades

The tradition of community organizing in Flint is long, storied, and rich. In 1936 and 1937, **striking** laborers at Flint's GM plant won a major victory for workers' rights. For 2 months, workers sat in one of the buildings and refused to leave. This strike empowered the United Auto Workers (UAW) **union**. The strike led to a 5 percent raise for workers and the right to **collectively bargain** with employers. Union membership in the United States ballooned as a result of the win.

Later, during the civil rights movement, Flint activists paved the way for equal housing rights. A "sleep-in" in August 1967 drew hundreds who demanded an end to racial discrimination in housing. Activist efforts continued. The next spring, voters in the city approved an open housing **referendum**. This opened up neighborhoods and housing to Black families. It was the first place in the country to make housing segregation illegal.

This civic tradition continued into the 21st century. When control of the city was turned over to an **emergency manager**, the Flint Democracy Defense League formed. And when the water crisis surfaced, these activists stood up and helped when the government failed, distributing bottled water to residents in need.

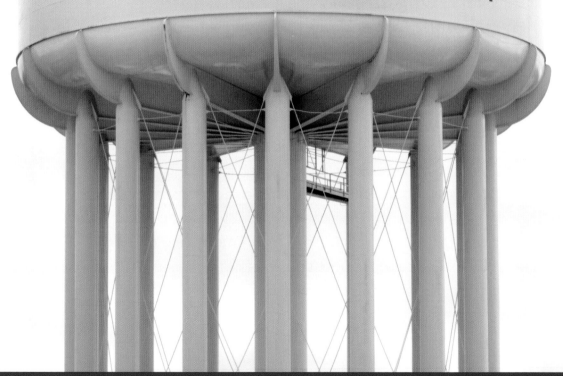

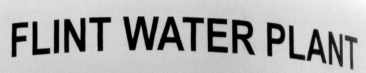

Flint's Water Treatment Plant was constructed in 1952.

and water. Those who remained in the city—whether by choice or by necessity—saw property taxes and water prices increase.

As a result, residents of Flint were paying among the highest water rates in the country by the 2010s. Before 2014, that water came from Lake Huron and was piped to the city by Detroit Water and Sewer. But in a move to save money for the struggling town, Flint's emergency manager decided to switch the water source. A deal that promised to save $200 million over 25 years was signed with a new provider, the Karegnondi Water Authority (KWA). However, the KWA water—also sourced from Lake Huron—wouldn't be available for a few years. In the meantime, Flint would get its water from the Flint River. It would be processed at an aging treatment facility.

CHAPTER 2

The Crisis

Within weeks of the switch, Flint residents grew suspicious of the water. It was discolored. It smelled terrible. It tasted disgusting. Officials told people not to worry. They assured them that the water was safe. But the reality was different. The strange color, odor, and taste of the water were symptoms of a bigger problem with the city's **corroded** pipes. What residents were seeing, smelling, and tasting were metals like iron.

In April of 2016, eight-year-old Mari Copeny sent a letter to President Obama. Known as "Little Miss Flint," Mari wrote, "I've been doing my best to march in protest and to speak out for all the kids that live here in Flint." President Obama sent an enthusiastic reply, noting that he'd soon be visiting the city and would welcome the chance to meet. Since that encounter, Mari Copeny has continued her environmental justice activism in and beyond her community.

Some water pipes in the United States are over 150 years old!

The Red Cross helped distribute bottled water and filters to Flint families.

Why were metals suddenly leaching into the water? When Flint authorities flipped the switch from lake to river water, they failed to do a few key things. First, they didn't treat the water with chemical additives called **orthophosphates**. These add a protective coating to aging pipes that controls corrosion. The river water had high levels of corrosives like chloride and salt in it from de-icing winter roadways, so it quickly began to eat away at the metal. On top of that, **chlorine**, which is added to city water to kill bacteria, had a chemical reaction with iron, preventing the chlorine from doing its job. This allowed harmful bacteria like *E. coli* and *Legionella* to thrive. By August 2014, just 4 months after changing the water source, Flint faced an *E. coli* outbreak. This was the first of many water issues to come.

Flint's government and economy were failing in the early 2000s. About 43 percent of its residents lived in poverty, and 13 percent of people under 65 didn't have health insurance. With a shrinking population, the city lacked resources to provide critical services, including infrastructure upkeep and maintenance.

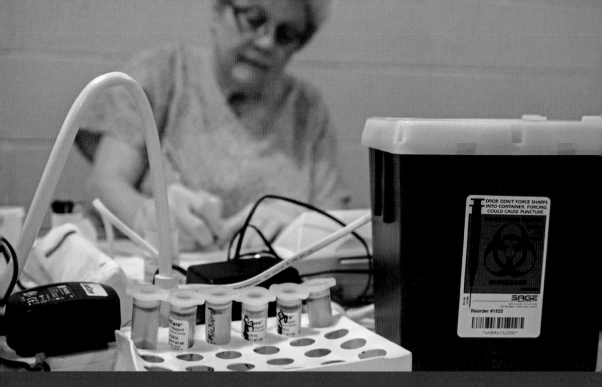

Medical technicians tested blood samples of Flint residents for lead.

You can see and taste iron, but you can't see or taste lead. So for months, residents had no idea of the danger. In January 2015, the University of Michigan-Flint detected lead in its water. Soon after, a city test found alarming levels in the home of resident LeeAnne

After the switch, the water in Flint was so corrosive that GM workers noticed it was causing their equipment to rust. The automaker changed back to its previous water source, provided by Detroit.

Walters, but officials dismissed it as an issue that just impacted her house. Walters then had her son's blood tested and learned he had lead poisoning. She contacted the Environmental Protection Agency (EPA), and Miguel del Toro, an employee at the EPA's Chicago office, sounded alarm bells. But no immediate action was taken.

Del Toro also gave Walters contact information for Marc Edwards, an environmental engineering professor at Virginia Tech. Edwards had previously worked to expose lead contamination in Washington, D.C. Walters thought he might be able to help prove that there was a real problem in Flint. Edwards immediately agreed.

In addition to community activists and scientists, investigative journalists also helped expose the Flint lead crisis. Curt Guyette, a reporter for the American Civil Liberties Union's Michigan office, demanded that people pay attention to the issue through his writing and a series of documentary films.

In September, fed-up community members in search of answers worked alongside Edwards and Virginia Tech students. They collected hundreds of water samples. The tests they ran showed that 20 percent of Flint's homes had too much lead. On September 24, Flint pediatrician Mona Hanna-Attisha revealed data showing that

A woman holds a baby bottle filled with Flint tap water.

lead levels in children's blood had increased since the water switch. According to her study, nearly 9,000 children under age 6 were exposed to lead-contaminated water.

With evidence mounting, the city issued a lead advisory to residents the next day. In early October, residents were given water filters and test kits. On October 16, it was announced that Flint would switch back to Detroit water. But the crisis was far from over.

On December 14, Flint mayor Karen Weaver declared a state of emergency. In January 2016, the state of Michigan and **federal** government did the same. Michigan governor Rick Snyder shared more alarming news. The water in Flint was the source of an outbreak of Legionnaires' disease, which had claimed at least 12 lives. This bacterial disease causes severe **pneumonia**. While 90 percent of cases are treatable with antibiotics, it can have lasting health effects. With at least 87 cases, Flint's outbreak was the third largest in U.S. history. This tragedy, paired with the lead crisis, left many wondering what was next for Flint.

What Lead Does to the Body

It's found in old windows, old paint, and old toys. It's durable and bendable, and it was widely used to make pipes from Roman times to the late 19th and early 20th centuries.

It's **element** 82, lead.

Since ancient Egypt—where it was used as makeup—people have been aware that lead can be toxic. When inhaled or swallowed, lead can cause a variety of symptoms and issues. These include behavior and learning problems, slowed growth, fatigue, and even **seizures**. In 2018, the leading medical journal *The Lancet* estimated that 400,000 U.S. deaths per year were caused by past exposure. For young children in particular, exposure can interfere with development.

How do people know if they have too much lead in their bodies? A simple blood test gives the answer.

CHAPTER 3

After

Five years after the water crisis, Dr. Hanna-Attisha told PBS *NewsHour*, "We can't take it away . . . we can't press rewind and pretend this didn't happen." While Flint's citizens are moving forward from the crisis, its impact still lingers. It's visible on city streets, where workers replace lead pipes with copper ones. It's evident in the court system, where residents fight to get compensated for harm. It's a painful, daily reality for those who lost loved ones to Legionnaires' disease. And it's a continuing concern for parents and teachers who want to make sure kids are growing and developing.

Flint's leaders hoped for a **comprehensive** disaster declaration from the federal government that would give more money for relief, but it didn't come. State and federal agencies' support, Medicaid assistance, corporate donations, and **nonprofit** and

During a visit to Flint in May 2016, President Barack Obama drinks water from the newly filtered system.

volunteer efforts helped rebuild the community. Local foundations worked tirelessly to provide early literacy, intervention services, and education to affected children. The University of Michigan-Flint offered a free course to educate the public on the crisis. Its aim was to promote understanding of the situation and to strategize solutions. Over 1,000 people attended.

Around the world, people who watched the water crisis wondered about justice. Would the decision-makers who kept information from the public be held **accountable**? That question is ongoing.

The cry for justice for Flint still can be heard today.

By the end of 2016, nine officials had been charged with crimes ranging from tampering with evidence to neglect of duty. But they all reached plea deals. In 2019, charges were dropped against the former director of Michigan's Department of Health and Human Services and the chief medical executive. Courts previously found both individuals guilty of **involuntary manslaughter**. Will there be a new investigation and retrial? That decision rests in the hands of the state's attorney general.

The crisis in Flint shone a spotlight on environmental injustice and "sacrifice zones." As the Center for Health, Environment and Justice notes, "Foul chemicals are not found equally everywhere in our country's air: They are highly concentrated in areas where people have lower incomes and are part of racial minority groups." The same goes for water and soil.

Today, activists around the world borrow from the tactics pioneered by Flint's citizen-scientists to build awareness and demand change. These activists showed that people can have power and exercise influence, even when officials want to deny it. In Michigan, this has brought about a strict new Lead and Copper Rule. It requires all lead service lines to be replaced by 2038.

The fight for environmental justice continues in communities across America. From ongoing struggles for clean soil and water on the Navajo Nation in Arizona to battles against the Keystone XL pipeline in the Midwest, concerned citizens are refusing to stay silent. In places large and small, rural and urban, people are working to prevent future unnatural disasters.

*The only time that federal disaster aid was given to a human-caused catastrophe was in 1978. The federal government stepped in during the Love Canal crisis in Niagara Falls, New York, to help **remediate** toxic chemicals. Since then, all disaster funds have been reserved for disasters of a natural sort, like hurricanes.*

Research & Act

Many young residents of Flint are quick to point out that the picture of their city painted by the media isn't complete. These tweens and teens use art and poetry to express their own thoughts, opinions, and feelings. Their words show that real people of all ages are impacted by—and can impact—politics and policy. Teen poet Destiny Monet, who participates in the arts organization Raise It Up!, told PBS in March 2016:

> *"Poetry matters everywhere. Specifically, spoken word matters everywhere, and especially in places like Flint where people are being looked over and ignored. We need poetry here because it is a platform for our pain and the injustices we witness every day, whether it's here in Flint or all over the world. Poetry is a way to let the world know that we are here and we aren't going anywhere. [It's] a way to provide knowledge to the unknowing in hopes that the more we educate ourselves on the issues, the more we can collectively come up with some solutions."*

Research the tradition of activist poetry. Then, think about a concern in your community. How can you use poetry to educate yourself and others about the issue? Write a poem that calls out the problem and your feelings on it.

Timeline

▶ **April 25, 2014:** To save money, Flint switches its water supply source.

▶ **May 2014:** Residents mount first complaints about water quality.

▶ **August 2014:** *E. coli* bacteria is detected in Flint's water.

▶ **October 2014:** Automaker GM stops using Flint water because of corrosion.

▶ **January and February 2015:** Tests at the University of Michigan-Flint and at a residence show high lead levels.

▶ **April–July 2015:** EPA employees raise concerns about lead levels in Flint, but no immediate action is taken.

▶ **September 2015:** Virginia Tech researchers work with Flint's citizen-scientists to collect water samples; samples show extraordinarily high levels of lead.

▶ **September 24, 2015:** A local hospital study shows elevated lead levels in Flint's children.

▶ **October 16, 2015:** Flint switches back to water supplied by Detroit.

▶ **December 14, 2015:** Flint's mayor declares a state of emergency.

▶ **January 2016:** Michigan's governor and President Obama also declare a state of emergency in Flint.

▶ **January 13, 2016:** Governor Snyder announces that Flint had experienced a Legionnaires' disease outbreak over the course of a year and a half.

Further Research

Conklin, Elise, director. *From Flint: Voices of a Poisoned City.* Kanopy, Video Project, 2016.

Ellis, Abby, director. *Flint's Deadly Water.* PBS *Frontline*, Sept. 10, 2019, www.pbs.org/video/flints-deadly-water-pwsj3m/.

Labrecque, Ellen. *Clean Water.* Ann Arbor, MI: Cherry Lake Publishing, 2018.

Santos, Rita. *Our Water Supply.* New York, NY: Enslow Publishing, 2019.

Yang, John, and Rachel Wellford. *"Why Flint Residents Are Still Dealing with Water Worries, 5 Years after Lead Crisis."* PBS *News Hour,* Oct. 3, 2019, www.pbs.org/newshour/show/why-flint-residents-are-still-dealing-with-water-worries-5-years-after-lead-crisis.

Glossary

accountable (uh-KOUNT-uh-buhl) responsible for an action or event

chlorine (KLOR-een) a chemical commonly added to water to kill bacteria

collectively bargain (kuh-LEK-tiv-lee BAHR-guhn) when a group of employees negotiates wages and benefits with an employer

comprehensive (kahm-prih-HEN-siv) complete, total

corroded (kuh-ROH-did) destroyed or damaged by a chemical action

downsized (DOUN-sized) reduced in size, such as the number of employees

E. coli (EE KOH-lye) bacteria sometimes found in contaminated food and water that can cause illness

element (EL-uh-muhnt) a basic unit of matter

emergency manager (ih-MUR-juhn-see MAN-ih-jur) a person appointed to oversee a struggling city's finances and government

federal (FED-ur-uhl) the central, as opposed to local or state, government

infrastructure (IN-fruh-struht-chur) basic and essential structures like roads, buildings, and sewage systems

involuntary manslaughter (in-VAH-luhn-ter-ee MAN-slaw-tur) the unlawful, accidental killing of another human being

leaching (LEECH-ing) dissolving

lead (LED) a toxic chemical that can cause severe damage when inhaled or ingested

Legionella (lee-juh-NEH-luh) bacteria that causes Legionnaires' disease and can lead to pneumonia

natural resources (NACH-ur-uhl REE-sors-iz) resources that exist in nature, like oil, coal, wood, and sun

nonprofit (nahn-PRAH-fit) an organization that serves the public good and does not exist solely to make profit

orthophosphates (or-thuh-FAHS-fates) chemicals that help form a protective coating on pipe walls

pneumonia (noo-MOHN-yuh) a potentially life-threatening lung infection

referendum (ref-uh-REN-duhm) a public vote on an issue or political question

remediate (rih-MEE-dee-ate) to fix or correct

seizures (SEE-zhurz) sudden brain disturbances that can lead to changes in behavior, movements, and feelings

striking (STRIKE-ing) refusing to work in order to get better conditions and wages

union (YOON-yuhn) an organized association of workers

INDEX

[21ST CENTURY SKILLS LIBRARY]